The Vietnam Conflict, 1945–75
Supplement Work Book
Full of Questions, Exam Technique and Tips.

By Alex Kerr

Edited by Liberal Publishing House

Complete Book: First Edition

'Those who fail to learn from History, are forced to repeat it.'

The last message to Washington from Saigon in 1975, from CIA Chief Thomas Polgar.

Preface:

This book intends to give as much information as possible about the history of warfare and to relate it to the IGCSE Edexcel exam board.

Alex Kerr has been teaching History and Politics for ten years. He is a graduate of Oxford Brookes University and has completed a PGCE at The Institute of Education, London as well as recently completing courses at the Johann Cruyff Institute, Barcelona.

The book will cover:

The first Indochina war

The second Indochina war, also known as the Vietnam Conflict or the Vietnam War.

This is an investigation study, so key aspects need to be learnt.

1.   The struggle against France for independence, 1945–54

2.   US policy and intervention, 1954–64

3.   Confrontation in the Vietnam War, escalation 1964–68

4.   Nixon and Ford's policies: Vietnamisation, peace & Communist victory, 1969–75

5.   The impact of conflict on civilians in Vietnam & attitudes in the USA

It is also divided into three question types:

(a): Wants the student to describe two key features of events or policies that took place during the Vietnam Conflict.

(b): How far does Source A support the evidence of Source B

(c): This question requires you to answer the question using all three sources and you must use all three sources and some of your own knowledge to gain full marks.

Contents:

Let's get started:

When you think of Vietnam, what do you think of?

Where is the country?

What is the significance of the country today?

What is the political background?

Well, a lot of it is connected to the Vietnam Conflict or War, which started from 1945 to 1975. However, for the Vietnamese, this was a war that had been going back even further. They were occupied by the Japanese during WW2 and before that, they were occupied by the French. The French had been operating in the area from around the 1600s and they had slowly but surely taken over the country and established a government and Catholicism as a religion in the area. For the Vietnamese, the war against a foreign army was nothing new.

Tour guide getting into one of the old Viet Cong tunnels.

Coalition: group of countries fighting together

Guerrilla: a type of war, including tactics such as hit and run. Small groups, rather than large armies, attack when the enemy is weak.

Sabotage: destroying something, e.g. power lines, pipelines

Terrain: the land, e.g. mountains, jungle, forest etc

Morale: the enthusiasm of people

Booby traps: traps for soldiers (fall into a spiked pit etc.) often set-off by a wire

Search and destroy: Tactic used by the US in Vietnam. Helicopters bring in soldiers, they attack a specific area such as a village, then leave

Rolling Thunder: name is giving to the bombing of North Vietnam by US Stealth aircraft planes that avoid being seen by radars.

Napalm: a petrol-based chemical used to kill people.

Colonialism: The idea of invading a country and putting it under the invading army's control.

Containment: The American idea of stopping the spread of Communism.

Domino Theory: The idea that if one country becomes Communist others nearby countries would become Communist as well.

United Nations: An organisation where nations from around the world can meet, debate and work on diplomacy to resolve conflict.

Capitalism: The idea of goods and services being exchanged for money, and a hierarchical society being acceptable.

Democracy: Greek for, The rule of people or people power. The idea that people vote for other people to represent their views.

Insurgent: A person who comes into a country to cause military or political disruption to its government.

Communism: The belief and political theory that all people should be equal in society, that there should be no government, no money, no private property, a 3-day working week and that people should be provided with what they need.

Conscription/draft: People being forced to join the nation's military.

ARVN: The Army of the Republic of Vietnam, created by the Americans and the Diem government.

CIA: Central Intelligence Agency is an American intelligence service, with the aim of gathering, processing, and analysing information from around the world,

Cadre: Trained and dedicated Communist Party Workers who organised resistance in South Vietnam's countryside and cities.

NVA: The North Vietnamese Army was founded by Ho Chi Minh in 1944, to attack the Japanese and then South Vietnam and America.

NLF: National Liberation Front was created under Le Duan and his supports in 1960. Their aim was to get rid of the Southern Government of Vietnam and the foreigners that supported him.

PLF: Peoples Liberation Armed Forces were the military side of the NFL and would become known as the Viet Cong.

Viet Cong: A communist political organization in South Vietnam, who used Guerrilla tactics.

Ho Chi Minh:

He adopted 70 different names in his life time. The final name means 'Enlightened one.' Born in 1890, exiled and lived in Paris, London, where he discovered Lenin and Communism, then to Moscow for Soviet training. He returned to China, developed a pro Vietnamese Communist group. He returned in 1941 and created the Viet Minh.

Le Duc Tho:

A North Vietnamese representative at secret negotiations with the United States and Henry Kissinger. He was a revolutionary veteran with 40 years' experience. He was awarded the Noble Peace prize in 1973 for his efforts in bringing peace between North Vietnam and America.

General Gaip:

General of the North Vietnam Armies who was original a French teacher. He converted to Communism after the French beat his wife to death in prison.

Le Duan:

Son of a carpenter, he founded the Indochinese Communist Party. Survived ten years in a French prison. He gained influence in the North Vietnamese politburo and began to change its policy. He argued that everything should be done to support the South Vietnamese, which was going against Ho Chi Minh's cautionary policy, to reunify the country. This policy encouraged North Vietnamese to move south along the Ho Chi Minh trail.

Ngo Dinh Diem:

A Catholic and Confucian he had travelled abroad seeking support for his version of democracy. He hated the French and the Communists. He had suffered because of the communists, who had imprisoned him, and buried alive his eldest brother and nephew. Diem was able to gain power in South Vietnam through rigged

Trần Lệ Xuân/Madam Nhu:

Wife of Ngo Dinh Nhu, considered to be a significant power in the South Vietnamese Diem regime, continually said inflammatory comments throughout the regime. She died in 2011.

Ngo Dinh Nhu:

The brother of Diem oversaw the South Vietnamese government and the secret police of south Vietnam. He helped his brother gain power of South Vietnam in 1955. He died in 1963 after a South Vietnamese military coup.

General de Lattre:

Commander of the French armies in Vietnam from 1950-1951. Born in 1889 and died in 1962. He oversaw Dien Bien Phu but was no longer in charge before its collapse.

President Truman:

President of the United States from 1945 – 1953, strong anti-communist views. He initiated the events in Vietnam with support for the French in holding the colony.

President Eisenhower:

President of the United States from 1953 to 1961. He continued the major aid to the French and the South Vietnam government. He led the formation of the Southeast Asia Treaty Organization. It was an alliance with Britain, France, New Zealand and Australia, with the aim of defending Vietnam and stopping communism.

President Kennedy:

President of the United States from 1961 to 1963. He continued the major aid to the South Vietnam government. Including increasing Military Advisors and Commandos.

President Johnson:

President of the United States from 1963 to 1969. He became president after the assassination of President Kennedy. He led huge welfare programs during his presidency as well as significant civil rights acts. In Vietnam and foreign affairs, he had kept President Kennedy's staff.

He continues to hope that America's will to persevere can be broken. Well, he is wrong.'

President Nixon:

President of the United States from 1969 to 1974. He had also been Vice-President under President Eisenhower. He caused the first peace talks to collapse before he was President. He promoted the idea of removing troops from Vietnam, and yet escalated the war in Cambodia and Laos.

President Ford:

President of the United States from 1974 – 1977. He was President during the final days of Saigon. Attempted to get funding from Congress to support the South Vietnamese government but was unable to achieve this.

Robert McNamara:

He was United States Secretary of Defence from 1961 – 1968. He had aimed at controlling and organising the war through statistics.

Henry Kissinger:

He was key to the peace agreements succeeding between the Americans and North Vietnamese allowing the Americans to withdraw from South Vietnam. He was awarded the Noble Peace prize in 1973. However, in 1975 after the fall of Saigon Kissinger tried to take the award back

General Westmoreland:
Commander of the Vietnam War from 1964 – 1968 and followed a similar belief to Robert McNamara that the war was to be won through statistics and that the real aim was to kill more people North Vietnamese than they could kill.

12

Timeline

1945

Ho Chi Minh creates a Provisional Government

Ho declares Vietnam independent

Britain lands troops in Saigon,

Britain returns authority to France

First American dies in Vietnam

1946

France and Viet Minh reach agreements

Agreements between France and Vietminh Breakdown

Indochina War starts

1947

Vietminh move north of Hanoi

1950

China and the Soviet Union (Russia today) offer weapons to Viet Minh

The US pledges $15M in aid to France

© 2018 Alex Kerr

1953

France grants Laos independence

Viet Minh troops enter into Laos

1954

Battle of Dien Bien Phu starts

Eisenhower discusses "Domino Theory" in regard to Southeast Asia

France defeated at Dien Bien Phu

Geneva Convention begins

Geneva Convention Agreements announced

1955

President of South Vietnam, Diem rejects the Geneva Accords and refuses to participate in Elections or Referendum for a united Vietnam.

China and Soviet Union pledge further financial support to North Vietnam.

1956

France leaves Vietnam

The US begins training South Vietnamese Troops

1957

Communists begin to come into South Vietnam. (Also known as Insurgency)

Saigon suffers from terrorist bombings from Viet Minh.

1959

Ho Chi Minh Trail starts to have weapons and supplies coming down it to support South Vietnamese Communists.

US Servicemen are killed in a guerrilla attack

President Diem begins crackdown of communists, Buddhists, gangs and opposition.

1960

North Vietnam starts military conscription

John F. Kennedy is elected President of the United States

President Diem survives first coup attempt

South Vietnamese create their own Communist political and military group known as the Viet Cong.

Y.A.F created.

1961

Vice President of the United States Johnson visits Saigon.

1962

US Military begins to use Agent Orange

South Vietnam's Presidential Palace bombed in another coup attempt

1963

President Kennedy assassinated in Dallas; Lyndon Johnson becomes president.

Buddhists protest Diem government by burning themselves and public demonstrations.

President Diem and his brother Nhu are overthrown and murdered. Nhu's wife escapes as she is in the U.S.

1964

General Nguyen Khanh Seizes Power in Saigon

Gulf of Tonkin Incident

1965

Operation "Rolling Thunder" started

First American combat troops arrive at Danang

US Troop Levels Top 200,000

Anti-war "Teach-In" protests broadcast to American Universities

1966

B-52s bombers bomb North Vietnam for the first time

South Vietnam Government troops take the cities of Hue and Danang

President Johnson meets with leaders of South Vietnamese

Veterans stage an Anti-War rally in Washington D.C.

1967

Dr Martin Luther King Speaks Out Against War

Robert McNamara states that the bombing is ineffective

Largest Pro-War rally held in New York.

1968

January

North Vietnam launches Tet Offensive

February

General Westmoreland requests 206,000 more troops

My Lai Massacre

March

President Johnson announces he won't run for a second term as president.

April

Dr King assassinated in Memphis.

May

Paris Peace Talks begin

August

Protests at the Democratic Convention in Chicago

September

NSCVV created.

November

Richard Nixon Elected President

1969

Nixon begins the secret bombing of Cambodia

"Vietnamization" started

Ho Chi Minh dies at the age of 79

News of My Lai Massacre reaches the US

Massive Anti-war Demonstration in DC

1970

Kent State Incident

Henry Kissinger & Le Duc start secret talks

The number of US troops reduced to 280,000

1971

Lt. Calley who was involved in the My Lai Massacre is convicted of Murder

The Pentagon Papers are published

Nixon announces he will visit China

1972

Nixon reduces the number of troops by 70,000

B-52s bomb Hanoi and Haiphong

The criminals breaking into the Watergate Hotel discovered and arrested

Kissinger announces "Peace Is At Hand"

Nixon wins a second term as President

1973

A cease-fire is signed in Paris

The United States announces that conscription/the draft has stopped

Last American troops leave Vietnam

Kissinger and Le Duc Tho both win the Noble Peace Prize

1974

President of South Vietnam, Thieu, announces the renewal of War

Communists take Mekong Delta Territory, which is north of Saigon

Nixon resigns as President

1975

The city of Hue captured by Communists

Ford announces the Vietnam War as "Finished"

Last Vietnam based American troops are killed

 Last Americans evacuate as Saigon Falls to Communists

<u>Helpful hints for students:</u>

North Vietnam General Giap stated that his Viet Cong guerrillas were:

"Everywhere and nowhere."

Chinese Communist Leader Mao Zedong summarised basic guerrilla tactics as:

"The enemy advances, we retreat; the enemy camps, we harass; the enemy tires, we attack; the enemy retreats, we pursue."

You will need to learn about the fundamental concepts relevant to this study:

Guerrilla warfare	Search and destroy	Hearts and Minds	Communist	Viet Cong Viet Minh N.L.F.	tactics
Domino Theory	A.R.V.N	Ho Chi Minh Trail	S.D.S.	strategy	technology

You are also going to have to learn about Key People

Le Duan	Ho Chi Minh	Diem	Richard Nixon	Lyndon Johnson	Westmoreland
McNamara	John Kennedy	Eisenhower	Truman	Ngo Diem	Madam Nhu
Kissinger	Ngo Dinh Nhu	De Lattre	Le Duc Tho	Ford	Giap

Two key terms to think about when answering these questions especially key feature questions is:

Significance: This is the influence or meaning of an impact on an event or the change the event has had. It can also be regarded as the importance of that impact. E.g. *The significance of 9/11 was that the West had to take the threat of terror attacks more seriously and change the approach to dealing with Islamic fundamentalism.*

Impact: This is how powerful the effect that something, especially some new change, has on a situation or person. E.g. *The use of the atom bomb had a tremendous impact on the superpowers because of this the Soviet Union retaliated by developing its own atomic weapons, and as a result, the arms race started.*

Chapter 1

The struggle against France for independence, 1945–54

What were the origins of the First Indochina War?

Step One:

List the five reasons below in order of Importance:

Ho Chi Minh, France, Communism, Colonialism and World War Two.

1. ....

2. ....

3. ....

4. ....

5. ....

Step Two:

Write why you put these events, people and philosophies in this order.

Ho Chi Minh, France, Communism, Colonialism and World War Two.

....

....

....

....

....

....

What was the name of the French defence tactic, named after an animal? Circle the correct Answer.

Hedgehog   Crocodile   Lion   Badger

What tactic did General de Lattre employ to stop the Viet Minh?

....

....

What did General Giap do in response to what General de Lattre had built?

....

....

Who won the battle of Dien Bien Phu? Circle the correct Answer.

France   Britain   America   Viet Minh

Can you name the 7 fortified points around the airstrip at Dien Bien Phu.?

1. ....

2. ....

3. ....

4. ....

5. ....

6. ....

7. ....

22

Using the Extract, how will the Viet Minh under General Giap attack the French at Dien Bien Phu?

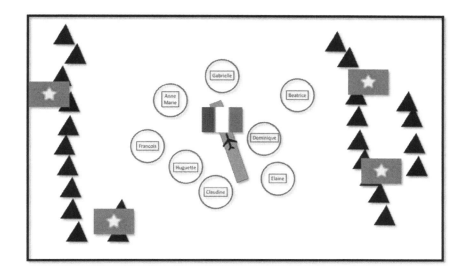

Come up with three reasons that the Viet Minh had success. You may reference the source.

....

....

....

....

....

....

How does this source/quote from Chinese Communist Leader Mao Zedong reflect the battle tactics of General Giap?

"The enemy advances, we retreat; the enemy camps, we harass; the enemy tires, we attack; the enemy retreats, we pursue."

There are at least two overall points to gain from this source/quote, which will reflect the nature of the combat for the rest of the Vietnam Conflict.

....

....

....

....

....

....

What had happened in Korea to cause the US to become more involved in Vietnam?

....

....

....

Some Source Work!

This is an important part of the exam, as two of the questions requires you look at the sources. One question requires you to compare the similarities and differences of the sources and then come to a conclusion. The conclusion is your own. You decide on whether the sources are similar or different, it is important that you come to a decision.

There are many great techniques out there to help you know how to tackle a source and find similarities and differences.

The one I use is COP.

Content

Origin

Purpose

What is the source talking about? Content

Where has the source come from? Origin = writer, newspaper, President, civilian.

What is the purpose of the source?

We also have sources and extracts. Sources are from the time period that you are studying. Extracts are from people not related to the event and have researched it.

So, Sources are your building blocks and the extract is the house.

The Sources are from the time, and you look at many, which helps to build a picture of the entire event. One civilian in North Vietnam giving a statement to the press cannot know what is happening around the rest of the country. Yet if there were statements from civilians around the country, we can begin to see what is happening, allowing us to build a picture of the events unfolding in the whole of Vietnam.

Source as drops of water and the extracts are the ocean.

So, let's check our use of COP. COP stands for?

C: ....

O: ....

P: ....

Now read this source: *Ho Chi Minh said about Korea in December 1953:*

"This is the first time (but not the last) that the United States has suffered a major defeat.... The current American scheme is to provoke wars in order to become master of the world.... The [French] enemy's primary design is 'to use Vietnamese to fight Vietnamese and to use war to breed war.'... The United States is forcing France to become a puppet and plans to replace France at every step."

Why is this a source?

....

What is the content in this source? Or what is it talking about?

....

....

....

....

....

What is the origin in the source? Who wrote this?

....

....

....

What is the purpose of this source? Why is Ho Chi Minh saying what he is saying?

....

....

....

....

List five key traits of Guerrilla warfare using the mind map below.

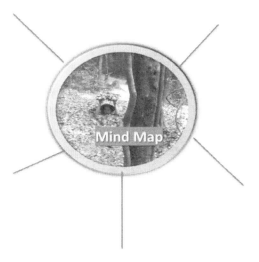

Use this page and mind map to recap on what you have learnt from the first Chapter:

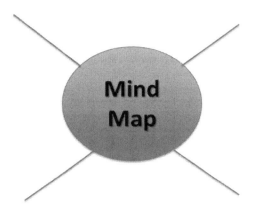

Chapter 2

US policy and intervention, 1954–64
Background:

The second part of the Vietnam war was between the ▦ USA and ▦ North Vietnam; other countries were also involved. By 1956, the French military had left Vietnam. It was started in secrecy and ended 30 years later in American failure. It witnessed by the entire World and involved 5 Presidents from both American political parties.

- ✖ More than 58,000 Americans were dead.
- ✖ An estimated 250,0000 South Vietnamese Soldiers died.
- ✖ 1 million North Vietnamese soldiers and Viet Cong.
- ✖ 2 million civilians across the whole of Vietnam as well as tens of thousands in Laos and Cambodia.

This war was over many different things. For some it was a civil war, for others it was a struggle for independence from foreign invasion. For the Americans involved, watching and protesting this would be one of the most divisive periods in American history. For others, the main point was the ideology. America, fearful of other countries becoming Communist, wanted to put a stop to it by using all its military might against the North Vietnamese, who were Communist.

The map on the next page shows the loose alliance system created after World War 2. The light blue represents capitalist countries and light red shows communist-run countries with ties to both China and the U.S.S.R. With the extremely light red showing countries with dictatorships. This period was known as the Cold War and would continue until the 1990s. Vietnam became a 'Hot Spot' of the Cold War and created a country for the Communists and Capitalists to fight each other directly and indirectly.

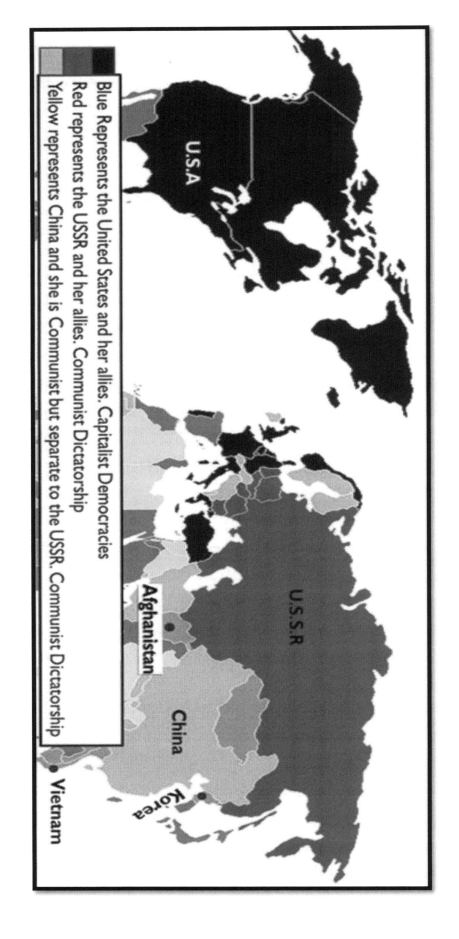

Blue Represents the United States and her allies. Capitalist Democracies

Red represents the USSR and her allies. Communist Dictatorship

Yellow represents China and she is Communist but separate to the USSR. Communist Dictatorship

U.S.A

Afghanistan

U.S.S.R

China

Korea

Vietnam

What were the aims of the Geneva Conference?

....

....

....

What were the results of the Geneva Conference?

1. ....

2. ....

3. ....

4. ....

What does this image show?

....

What does the image above mean to the USA?

....

....

....

....

....

What was the name of the US policy used to deal with the above concern? Circle the correct answer:

Containment   Search and Destroy   The Geneva Accords   Hearts & Minds

What happened on each of the dates below that would cause the United States to become more and more involved in the Vietnam Conflict?

1954...

....

....

....

....

1956...

....

....

....

1961...

....

....

....

1962 ....

....

....

....

....

1963 ....

....

....

....

....

Give 2 facts about each person

Ho Chi Minh

....

....

....

....

Ngo Dinh Diem

....

....

....

....

President Kennedy

....

....

....

....

Use the Mind Map to explain why the Viet Cong were a threat by 1964.

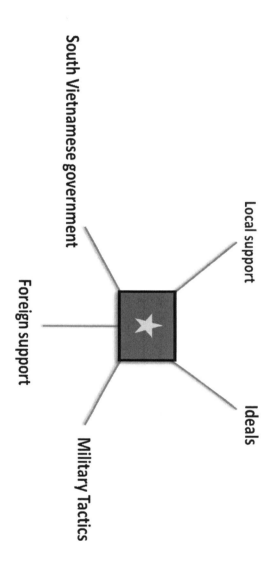

South Vietnamese government

Local support

Foreign support

Ideals

Military Tactics

History is about looking at both sides of an argument and coming to your own conclusions. Think about a reason, and then explain why it was a good thing. This is the basis of constructing any argument. Point + Explanation = a justified argument.

Give two positives about the South Vietnamese Government.

....

....

....

....

Give two negatives about the South Vietnamese Government.

....

....

....

....

What was the name of the Buddhist Martyr who set himself on fire?

Quang Duc   Duc Quang   Le Duc Tho   Le Duan

What was the purpose of the Ho Chi Minh trail? Give two reasons.

....

....

....

....

What countries did it run through?

1.

2.

3.

4.

What was the phrase used by the Viet Cong who worked on the Ho Chi Minh trail?

....

....

By 1964, an estimated 20-30 tons of supplies per day were being brought into South Vietnam using the Trail. How many tons were being brought in per day by the following year?

400   4000   234   345,000

What was the aim of the Strategic Hamlets programme?

....

....

How were the Strategic Hamlets meant to achieve this aim? Give two methods.

....

....

....

....

State two reasons why the Strategic Hamlets programme failed:

....

....

....

....

....

....

....

....

How many incidents took place in the Gulf of Tonkin?

1   2   3   4   5   6

What creature did President Johnson refer to in this quote about the Gulf of Tonkin Incident?

"For all I know, our navy was shooting at .... out there."

Circle the correct answer:

Whales   Sharks   Gorillas   Dolphins

What did the Gulf of Tonkin incidents cause the United States to do?

....

....

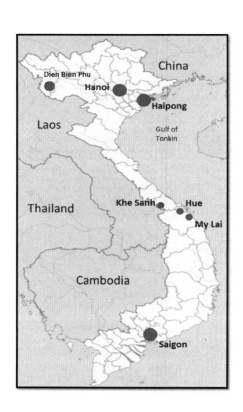

"I have never talked or corresponded with a person knowledgeable in Indochinese affairs who did not agree that had elections been held as of the time of the fighting, possibly 80% of the population would have voted for the Communist Ho Chi Minh as their leader rather than Chief of State Bảo Đại. Indeed, the lack of leadership and drive on the part of Bảo Đại was a factor in the feeling prevalent among Vietnamese that they had nothing to fight for."

So, let's check our use of COP. COP stands for?

C: ....

O: ....

P: ....

Now read this source: President Eisenhower stated:

"I have never talked or corresponded with a person knowledgeable in Indochinese affairs who did not agree that had elections been held as of the time of the fighting, possibly 80% of the population would have voted for the Communist Ho Chi Minh as their leader rather than Chief of State Bảo Đại. Indeed, the lack of leadership and drive on the part of Bảo Đại was a factor in the feeling prevalent among Vietnamese that they had nothing to fight for."

What is the content in this source? Or what is it talking about?

....

....

....

....

....

What is the origin in the source? Who wrote this?

....

....

....

What is the purpose of this source? Why is Ho Chi Minh saying what he is saying?

....

....

....

....

For the second question, we need to look at comparing two sources. So that means you must look at the similarities and the differences, and then conclude as to whether you think they are similar or different.

From a speech by President Eisenhower to Congress, April 1954.

You now have a row of dominoes set. You knock over the first one. What will happen to the last one is the certainty that it will go over very quickly. More people have already come under communist domination. Asia has already lost some 450 million of its peoples to the communist dictatorship. We simply can't afford even greater losses of materials and millions and millions more people to communism.

Source B: From a speech by President Johnson to Congress, 5 August 1964.

The threat to the free nations of Southeast Asia has long been clear. The North Vietnamese regime has constantly tried to take over South Vietnam and Laos. As President of the United States, I ask Congress to support me in making clear the determination of the US: such threats will be opposed. The United States will continue in its basic policy of assisting the free nations of the area to defend their freedom.

So, first things first. Try out COP.

One of the things I instruct students to do is to look at the text, then go over it again with a highlighter.

From a speech by President Eisenhower to Congress, April 1954.

You now have a row of dominoes set. You knock over the first one. What will happen to the last one is the certainty that it will go over very quickly. More people have already come under communist domination. Asia has already lost some 450 million of its peoples to the communist dictatorship. We simply can't afford even greater losses of materials and millions and millions more people to communism.

Note I have also highlighted the 'Origin' part of the text.

Now you try with a highlighter.

Source B: From a speech by President Johnson to Congress, 5 August 1964.

The threat to the free nations of Southeast Asia has long been clear. The North Vietnamese regime has constantly tried to take over South Vietnam and Laos. As President of the United States, I ask Congress to support me in making clear the determination of the US: such threats will be opposed. The United States will continue in its basic policy of assisting the free nations of the area to defend their freedom.

Once you have highlighted and read through both sources you need to answer the question:

How far does Source A support the evidence of Source B about US policy in Vietnam?

Explain your answer.

You could start your opinion in the first sentence and state that you think they do or do not support each other.

Then you will need to show from the sources where they are supporting each other.

They both certainly talk about threats. You would need to reference both sources on where they both talk about threats and explain why they are the same.

You would then need to state where they do not agree with one another.

So, use the word. 'However,', or 'Yet,' or 'Nevertheless,' to show the opposing side of the argument.

Now you go through the sources and see where you can find parts of the source where they differ. It might be in what they say or what one source talks about and the other does not talk about. There is space to write on the next page.

For extra help:

Here is what the examiners are asked to look for when marking your papers:

"Answer provides an explained evaluation of the extent of support. The sources are cross referenced, and comparisons used to support reasoning about the extent of support."

Use this page and mind map to recap on what you have learnt from the Second Chapter:

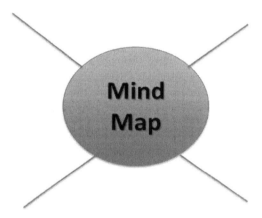

Chapter 3

Confrontation in the Vietnam War, escalation 1964–68

Events:

The Gulf of Tonkin was the final piece for the full escalation of the war and bringing America into the Vietnam Conflict. Yet no declaration of war was made, however, Congress did pass the Tonkin Gulf Resolution. The Tonkin Gulf Resolution in 1964 gave the President the powers to send America to war, but it was not a declaration of war. The Americans began a bombing campaign against North Vietnam and the Ho Chi Minh trail.

The Viet Cong was the name of the Communist guerrilla army who were partly from the south of Vietnam and from north Vietnam. They mainly used guerrilla tactics to fight because they could not match the strength of the US military, its resources and equipment. The North Vietnamese Army (NVA) and Viet Cong were no match for the USA and the Army of the Republic of Vietnam (ARVN) in open warfare.

Learn these spellings (ARVN, Ho Chi Minh, Trail, Viet Cong & NFL) and use them correctly in a sentence in the space provided.

ARVN

Ho Chi Minh Trail

Viet Cong

N.F.L.

What are the names of these three men?

1.

2.

3.

What position did each of these men have?

1.

2.

3.

Why were tactics like Search and Destroy likely to alienate and upset the local population?
Use the image like a mind map to think of reasons

50

Place these events, dates and details in some order. You can use a highlighter to colour code them so that the date, event and consequence are matched.

Event	Date	Details
Thích Quảng Đức	1966-1967	*Two events at sea that were to cause the beginning of direct American military involvement in Vietnam.*
The Tet Offensive is launched by the Vietcong.	*June 1963*	An attempt to prevent supplies being transported on the Ho Chi Minh Trail
Start of Operation Rolling Thunder	March 1965	Over 500, 000 men died within 3 years of this decision
Search and Destroy (Zippo raids)	Jan 1968	Although the VC lost more soldiers, the humiliation of the events led to increased opposition to the war in the USA.
Ground troops were sent into Vietnam.	Feb 1965	A program started by General Westmoreland in his efforts to stop the Viet Cong.
Gulf of Tonkin Incident	1964	This monk set himself on fire because of the missed treatment of Buddhists in South Vietnam.

Choose two reasons why the Tet Offensives were effective for the Viet Cong.

....

....

....

....

....

....

....

Choose two reasons why the Tet Offensives were not effective for the Viet Cong.

....

....

....

....

....

....

....

The image shows the US Embassy in Saigon. Label the picture with reasons why the Tet Offensive came as a shock to the US public

Write two facts about each individual, event or group:

The battle of Hue:

....

....

....

....

The battle of Khe Sanh:

....

....

....

....

Walter Cronkite:

....

....

....

....

54

National Liberation Front:

....

....

....

....

Robert McNamara:

....

....

....

....

Le Duan:

....

....

....

....

American news reporter Neil Sheehan, who had visited Vietnam with Robert McNamara:

'I remember going, during one of Robert McNamara's visits, out to one of these hamlets. The Vietnamese General who commanded the area was telling McNamara what a wonderful thing this was. And some of these farmers were digging a ditch around the hamlet. And I looked at their faces and they were really angry. I mean, it was very obvious to me that if these people could, they'd cut our throats.'

Stanley Karnow, an American Historian and Journalist wrote:

From the start, in Hoa Phu and elsewhere, they had hated the strategic hamlets, many of which they had been forced to construct by corrupt officials who had pocketed a percentage of the money allocated for the projects. Besides, there were virtually no government troops in the sector to keep them from leaving. If the war was a battle for "hearts and minds,"...the United States and its South Vietnamese clients had certainly lost

Once you have highlighted and read through both sources you need to answer the question:

How far does Source A support the evidence of Source B about the success of the Strategy Hamlet Programme in Vietnam?

Remember.

You could start your opinion in the first sentence and state that you think they do or do not support each other.

Then you will need to show from the sources where they are supporting each other.

They both certainly talk about threats. You would need to reference both sources on where they both talk about threats and explain why they are the same.

You would then need to state where they do not agree with one another.

So, use the word. 'However,', or 'Yet,' or 'Nevertheless,' to show the opposing side of the argument.

There is space to write on the next page.

For extra help:

Here is what the examiners are asked to look for when marking your papers:

"Answer provides an explained evaluation of the extent of support. The sources are cross referenced, and comparisons used to support reasoning about the extent of support."

57

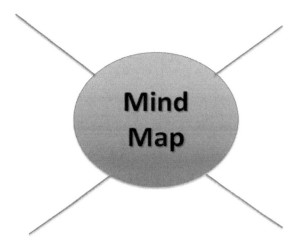

Chapter 4

Nixon and Ford's policies, Vietnamisation, peace and Communist victory 1969–75

'The killing in this tragic war must stop.' President Nixon

A poster from the 1960s Presidential elections.

By 1968 there were over half a million US troops were in Vietnam.

The US army was not able to defeat the communists with their superior knowledge of the land and support from the people. At this point, the American public was opposed to the war and began to protest.

Many American troops were being killed or injured and this contributed to a strong anti-war feeling in the USA.

Richard Nixon, an experienced politician, including 8 years as Vice-President under President Eisenhower managed to become President of the United States in 1968. He had campaigned on the promise of stopping the Vietnam Conflict. The new President decided to replace US troops with South Vietnamese soldiers, but this still did not defeat the Viet Cong. In 1973 a peace agreement was signed between the USA and North Vietnam which ended the war. In 1975 the communists defeated the South and the whole country became communist.

General Recap:

Give two facts for each question:

What was the domino theory?

....

....

....

....

What was a strategic hamlet?

....

....

....

....

What happened as a result of the Gulf of Tonkin incident?

....

....

....

....

What was Operation Rolling Thunder?

....

....

....

....

Why did President Johnson first send ground troops to Vietnam?

....

....

....

....

Why were Cambodia and Laos were bombed in 1970 and 1971?

....

....

....

....

What were the key features of Vietnamization?

Why did the Paris Peace talks fail?

Give two reasons.

....

....

....

....

What pressure was placed on Vietnam by Nixon's visit to China?

....

....

....

....

The Dove is a peace symbol. Using the dove below explain the reasons for the secret peace negotiations being successful.

What were the names of the Two men having secret peace agreements in Paris?

Kissinger   Le Duc Tho   Le Duan   Ho Chi Minh

Nixon   McNamara   Johnson   Westmoreland

Why did Nixon resign from being President? Give one reason.

....

....

....

....

How did President Ford respond to the Vietnam Conflict: Give two features?

....

....

....

....

....

....

....

....

Source A: From a speech by President Eisenhower to Congress, April 1954.

You now have a row of dominoes set. You knock over the first one. What will happen to the last one is the certainty that it will go over very quickly. More people have already come under communist domination. Asia has already lost some 450 million of its peoples to the communist dictatorship. We simply can't afford even greater losses of materials and millions and millions of more people to communism.

Source B: From a speech by President Johnson to Congress, 5 August 1964.

The threat to the free nations of Southeast Asia has long been clear. The North Vietnamese regime has constantly tried to take over South Vietnam and Laos. As President of the United States, I ask Congress to support me in making clear the determination of the US: such threats will be opposed. The United States will continue in its basic policy of assisting the free nations of the area to defend their freedom.

Extract C: From A History of the Modern World, published in 1996.

The main reason for American involvement in South Vietnam was the increased threat from the Vietcong. By 1961, the Vietcong forces were being supported with troops and weapons supplied by Ho Chi Minh's government. As war within Vietnam escalated, President Kennedy sent in more military advisers. His successor, Lyndon Johnson, believed that it was vital to defeat communism in Vietnam. In August 1964, two American ships were fired on by North Vietnamese gunboats in the Gulf of Tonkin. President Johnson persuaded Congress to give him wide powers to expand the war.

Extract C suggests that the main reason for increased US involvement in Vietnam in the years 1954–64 was the threat from the Vietcong.

How far do you agree with this interpretation?

Use Extract C, Sources A and B and your own knowledge to explain your answer.

(16)

To answer this question, you are going to need the techniques that I showed you earlier and the exam board has been nice in already helping you to analysis the two sources. The only thing left is to look at the extract and decide where it lands in relation to the question.

Get out the highlighter:

Extract C suggests that **the main reason** for increased US involvement in Vietnam in the years 1954–64 was the threat from the Viet Cong.

How far do you agree with this interpretation?

Use Extract C, Sources A and B and your own knowledge to explain your answer.

(16)

So, do sources A and B support this or do they have other reasons?

Do they mention the Viet Cong in any of the sources?

What do the sources mention as the main reason?

Then look at Extract C.

Does Extract C mention the Viet Cong?

What else does it mention?

Introductions

To get this essay correct you need a solid introduction to the essay.

This needs to the foundation of the essay and it needs to mention the sources, extract and if you can some of your own knowledge.

This is an example, and not necessarily the correct answer.

"Sources A and B disagree with the statement that the Viet Cong were the main reason for American involvement and the Gulf of Tonkin incident was not done by the Viet Cong but her allies.

However,

Extract C shows that the Viet Cong were clearly the main cause of American involvement and we can see this through the Gulf of Tonkin incident caused in part by the Viet Cong's allies."

History is a blurry debatable topic. You can have overlap and contradiction in your history, sources and extracts. In this case, we could look at the Gulf of Tonkin incident and say it was involved with the Viet Cong and we could argue that it was not.

North Vietnam supported and financed the Viet Cong. However, the Viet Cong could be considered a separate entity, as could be seen in the secret agreements with Kissinger and Le Duc Tho. These secret talks excluded the Viet Cong.

Main Body

After your introduction, you will need to go into the main body.

This will need to go into further detail about the sources, and your own knowledge.

Attempt to talk about the sources and answer the question about the Viet Cong. Then leave a couple of sentences referencing the sources and extract using COP and focusing on the origin and purpose because you should have already talked about the Content.

Then start the next paragraph with: "However,"

Talk about the other side of the argument. Reference the sources and extract if relevant.

Conclusion

Finally, a conclusion. What do you think? Was it the Viet Cong or was it something else? You decide and conclude.

"I think the Viet Cong were or were not the main cause…..

On the next page, I have left you some room to practice. Try to do this under timed conditions, to get the best practice possible. Don't forget practice makes perfect.

....

....

....

....

....

....

....

....

....

....

....

....

....

....

....

....

....

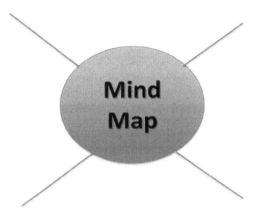

Chapter 5

The impact on civilians in Vietnam and attitudes in the USA

'People sing about Victory, about Liberation. They're wrong. In war, who won and who lost is not a question. In war, no one wins or loses. There is only destruction. Only those who have never fought like to argue about who won and who lost.' Bao Ninh, North Vietnamese Army.

Who were the SDS? Give two key features.

....

....

....

....

What was the draft? Give two key features.

....

....

....

....

Who was Lieutenant Calley?

....

....

What was the event that Lieutenant Calley responsible for?

....

....

What happened at Kent State University in 1970? Give two features.

....

....

....

....

Who asked for the support of the 'silent majority'? Give the name of the person only.

....

How many troops in total died in Vietnam?

....

Write up a mind map of as many events and people as you can think of related to the pro-war protests.

This is Lieutenant Calley and was involved in My Lai use the image to build a mind map.

How did the Kent State shooting effect the public? Make a mind map.

Give 5 reasons why opposition to the war in America increases?

Reason 1

....

....

....

....

Reason 2

....

....

....

....

Reason 3

....

....

....

....

Reason 4

....

....

....

....

Reason 5

....

....

....

....

Give two features of the Fulbright Hearings:

....

....

....

....

Which one of these two were not used to bomb Vietnam:

Agent Orange   Napalm   Agent Red   Bath Bomb

Use this page and mind map to recap on what you have learnt from the fifth Chapter:

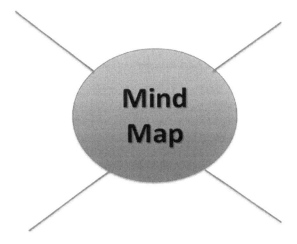

I have included sources and extracts on the following pages. This should allow you to practice C.O.P. or comparison work or to practice a three-way comparison essay.

Why the French lost:

"I am convinced that the French could not win the war because the internal political situation in Vietnam, weak and confused, badly weakened their military position. I have never talked or corresponded with a person knowledgeable in Indochinese affairs who did not agree that had elections been held as of the time of the fighting, possibly 80 per cent of the population would have voted for the Communist Ho Chi Minh as their leader rather than Chief of State Bao Dai. Indeed, the lack of leadership and drive on the part of Bao Dai was a factor in the feeling prevalent among Vietnamese that they had nothing to fight for."

Dwight D. Eisenhower, The White House Years (1963), vol. 1, p. 372.

Anti- War:

"Why should they ask me to put on a uniform and go 10,000 miles from home and drop bombs and bullets on Brown people in Vietnam while so-called Negro people in Louisville are treated like dogs and denied simple human rights? No I'm not going 10,000 miles from home to help murder and burn another poor nation simply to continue the domination of white slave masters of the darker people the world over."

Muhammad Ali

"The war is simply an obscenity, a depraved act by weak and miserable men, including all of us who have allowed it to go on and on with endless fury and destruction – all of us who would have remained silent had stability and order been secured."

Noam Chomsky, in American Power and the New Mandarins (1969), Introduction.

"To say that we are closer to victory today is to believe, in the face of the evidence, the optimists who have been wrong in the past. To suggest we are on the edge of defeat is to yield to unreasonable pessimism. To say that we are mired in stalemate seems the only realistic, if unsatisfactory, conclusion. On the off chance that military and political analysts are right, in the next few months we must test the enemy's intentions, in case this is indeed his last big gasp before negotiations. But it is increasingly clear to this reporter that the only rational way out then will be to negotiate, not as victors, but as an honorable people who lived up to their pledge to defend democracy and did the best they could."

Walter Cronkite, CBS TV news anchor, on "Report from Vietnam," aired February 27, 1968.

"I figured if this medal is so important let's make it important. Here it is. You can have it back. End the war in Vietnam. What else is there? There was nothing else. I wouldn't put them on the wall for my son. That was the last thing in the world I would ever want my son to revere."

Ron Ferrizzi quoted in The Vietnam War: An Intimate History by Geoffrey Ward and Ken Burns (2017), p. 481-3. Ferrizzi is recalling his participation in the anti-Vietnam protest where he threw his military medals onto the steps of Congress.

Why the Americans lost:

Patton asked him to go aboard a chopper equipped with a loudspeaker and order his men to surrender. The prisoner quickly refused, and Patton said to him, "If you don't go up in the chopper with me and ask them to surrender you have personally signed their death warrants, because I will be forced to obliterate this position." The NVA captain again declined, and Patton's frustration was evident. He glowered at the man, and said, "Goddamn it, who is winning this war?" "You are," was the reply. "Then in that case," Patton shouted, "why don't we save the lives of your soldiers and let us take them out and feed them and medicate them?" "Sir," he said, "you didn't ask who would win this war." "Well, who is going to win this war?" Patton snorted. "We will," the prisoner said forcefully, "because you will tire of it before we do."

Brian M. Sobel, quoting an exchange between an American officer serving in Vietnam, George Patton, and a North Vietnamese Army officer in December 1968, in his book The Fighting Pattons (1997), p. 167-168.

In 1971, The New York Times stated that the build-up to the Vietnam Conflict was achieved, *"with acts of sabotage and terror warfare against North Vietnam beginning in 1954; with moves that encouraged and abetted the over-throw of President Ngo Dinh Diem of South Vietnam in 1963; with plans, pledges and threats of further action that sprang to life in the Tonkin Gulf clashes in August, 1964; with the careful preparation of public opinion for the years of open warfare that were to follow; and with the calculation in 1965, as the planes and troops were openly committed to sustained combat, that neither accommodation inside South Vietnam nor early negotiations with North Vietnam would achieve the desired result."*

Increasing American Involvement:

In April 1965 a message was sent to Defense Secretary McNamara from CIA Director McCone:

". . . It is my judgment that if we are to change the mission of the ground forces, we must also change the ground rules of the strikes against North Vietnam. We must hit them harder, more frequently, and inflict greater damage. Instead of avoiding the MIG's, we must go in and take them out. A bridge here and there will not do the job. We must strike their airfields, their petroleum resources, power stations and their military compounds. This, in my opinion, must be done promptly and with minimum restraint."

"That the Truman Administration decision to give military aid to France in her colonial war against the Communist-led Vietminh "directly involved" the United States in Vietnam and "set" the course of American policy.

That the Eisenhower Administration's decision to rescue a fledgling South Vietnam from a Communist takeover and attempt to undermine the new Communist regime of North Vietnam gave the Administration a "direct role in the ultimate breakdown of the Geneva settlement" for Indochina in 1954.

That the Kennedy Administration, though ultimately spared from major escalation decisions by the death of its leader, transformed a policy of "limited-risk gamble," which it inherited, into a "broad commitment" that left President Johnson with a choice between more war and withdrawal."

New York Times, June 1971, based on the information found in the pentagon papers.

Involvement in getting rid of Nhu and Diem Government:

On August 23rd, the first contact with a U.S. representative was made by generals who had begun to plan a coup against Diem. The generals wanted a clear indication of where the U.S. stood. State in its subsequently controversial reply, drafted and cleared on a weekend when several of the principal Presidential advisors were absent from Washington, affirmed that Nhu's continuation in a power position within the regime was intolerable and, if after Diem had been given an opportunity to rid himself of Nhu and did not, "then we must face the possibility that Diem himself cannot be preserved."

Pentagon Papers. The Overthrow of Ngo Dinh Diem, May – Nov, 1963, page iii.

Tet Offensive:

"The enemy had achieved in South Vietnam neither military nor psychological victory. For the South Vietnamese the Tet offensive served as a unifying catalyst, a Pearl Harbor. Had it been the same for the American people, had President Johnson discerned the same support behind him that Thieu did behind him, and had he acted with forcefulness, the enemy could have been induced to engage in serious and meaningful negotiations. Unfortunately, the enemy scored in the United States the psychological victory that eluded him in Vietnam, so influencing President Johnson and his civilian advisors that they ignored the maxim that when the enemy is hurting, you don't diminish the pressure, you increase it."

General William Westmoreland, in his memoirs A Soldier Reports (1976), p. 334.

Peace with honor:

"Throughout the years of negotiations we have insisted on peace with honour. In the settlement that has now been agreed all these conditions have been met. The conditions include the release of prisoners of war within 60 days and all American forces to be withdrawn within the same time. To the people of South Vietnam, we say by your courage you have won the right to determine your own future. To the leaders of North Vietnam, as we have ended the war through negotiation, let us build a peace of reconciliation."

From a speech by President Nixon in January 1973 to the American people.

Kent State Shooting:

"They are shooting blanks, I thought. Then I heard a ping. I thought, 'My God, this is for real'. The shooting stopped. The campus was suddenly still. Then screams broke out. 'My God, they're killing us!' one girl cried. They were. A river of blood ran from the head of one boy, soaking his textbooks."

From an eye witness account by Professor Charles Brill, a member of Kent State University staff, May 1970.

Increasing American involvement:

"Johnson was equally determined to prevent the expansion of communism in Southeast Asia, but the price the United States had to pay in lives and money to do so would be much higher than in Latin America. Between November 1963 and July 1965, Johnson transformed Kennedy's program of limited U.S. assistance to South Vietnam into an open-ended commitment to defend that country. By 1968 the United States would have over 500,000 troops in Vietnam. Johnson believed, probably correctly, that South Vietnam would collapse if the United States did not expand its participation in the war."

Ronald Powaski, The Cold War: The United States and the Soviet Union, 1917-1991 (1998), p. 155

"The Eisenhower administration, which had refused to sign the Geneva Accords, feared a communist victory in the national elections and a domino effect throughout Southeast Asia. After the French withdrawal, the United States proceeded to build up a client state in the south, allowing President Ngô Đình Diệm to cancel the 1956 elections and to clamp down on his opponents.... Eisenhower expanded US economic and military aid and personnel on the ground. Between 1955 and 1961 the United States poured more than $1 billion in economic and military aid into the Diệm regime, and by the time Eisenhower left office there were approximately one thousand US military advisers in South Vietnam."

Carole C. Fink, Cold War: An International History (2017), p. 96-97

Although neither US ship had been hit and there were no casualties, Johnson immediately ordered a retaliatory bombing raid against North Vietnamese naval bases. Evoking America's dread of surprise assaults, Johnson appealed for public support against an "unprovoked attack" in international waters. After Defense Secretary Robert McNamara assured Congress that the US Navy had "played absolutely no part in, was not associated with, was not aware of any South Vietnamese actions, if there were any," Johnson on August 7, 1964 won near-unanimous Senate approval for a resolution authorizing him to use US military force to defend the freedom of South Vietnam,

Carole C. Fink, Cold War: An International History (2017), p. 126

Peace with honor:

1973- This was the year that the war finally ended. Nixon called it "peace with honor," although he surely knew that the Communists would take over, just the same as if we had never gotten involved over there in the first place- except of course for the hundreds of thousands of people who got hurt or killed. So you tell me why the whole thing was not a terrible, criminal waste. You tell me why Henry Kissinger got the Nobel Peace Prize, instead of being required- along with all the other "leaders" who kept sending Americans over there long after they knew the war was pointless- to get down on his knees and beg the forgiveness of the American veterans, and their families, and the Vietnamese people

Dave Barry, Dave Barry Turns 50 (1998), p. 151.

Why the Americans lost:

You know, we get involved in these wars and we don't know a damn thing about those countries, the culture, the history, the politics, people on top and even down below. And, my heavens, these are not wars like World War II and World War I, where you have battalions fighting battalions. These are wars that depend on knowledge of who the people are, with the culture is like. And we jumped into them without knowing.

Les Gelb interviewed on On the Media 2018

I have included a section for you to write notes or attempt to work on the sources, and

practice C.O.P.

....

....

....

....

....

....

....

....

....

....

....

....

....

....

....

....

Bibliography:

- The Pentagon Papers, Gravel Edition, (Boston: Beacon Press, 1971) Volume 1.
- *Vietnam: a History,* (Viking,1983) Stanley Karnow
- *Vietnam: An Epic Tragedy, 1945-1975, 1st Edition (Harper, 2018) Max Hastings*
- *Tonkin Gulf and the escalation of the Vietnam War, 1st Edition (University of North Carolina Press, 1996) Edwin Moise*
- *The Pro-War Movement: Domestic Support for the Vietnam War and the Making of Modern American Conservatism (Culture, Politics, and the Cold War) 1st Edition (University of Massachusetts Press, 2013) Sandra Scanlon*
- *The Vietnam War: An Intimate History (Knopf, 2017) by Ken Burns, Lynn Novick and Geoffrey Ward.*

Changing Nature of Warfare, 1918 - 2011

Complete Student Book: Full of Maps and Facts

Changing Nature of Warfare, 1918 - 2011,

Supplement Work Book: Full of Questions, Exam Technique and Tips.

Changing Nature of Warfare, 1918 - 2011,

Express Revision Work Book: Full of Questions, Exam Technique and Tips.

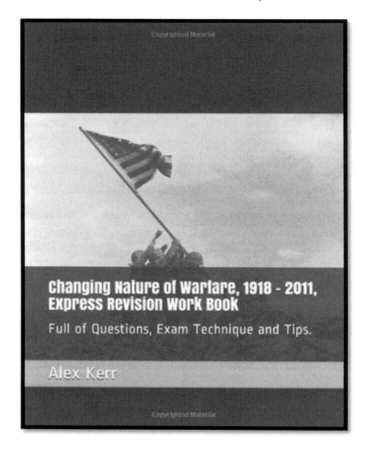

The Vietnam Conflict, 1945 - 75: IGCSE

Full of Maps and Facts.

Where should I stay in Sicily? Ortigia & Syracuse/Siracusa

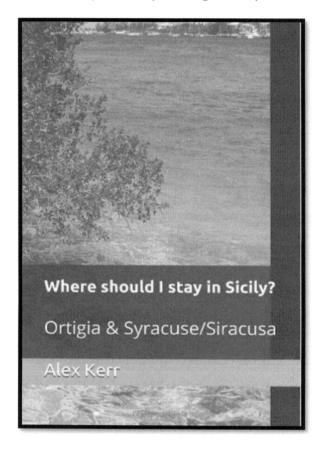

Printed in Great Britain
by Amazon